Celebrating Men
Companion
Group Discussion Guide

By

B. Niles

Published by B. Niles Books
Book Cover Design by Eugene Miti

ISBN 978-1460995556

Dedicated to:

The Memory of
Aundré Niles
and to all
Iraq Veterans

CONTENTS

INTRODUCTION

"God saw all that he made, and it was very good."
Genesis 1:31

The premise of *Celebrating Men* is that men need to be restored to their God-given position and relevance in their families, churches and communities. The position taken is a biblical one. Man was created in the image of God to be the head and priest of his household and to be a leader in his community. Man is the only animal, if you will, that God breathed life into. This unique action of creation demonstrated God's special love and care for man. God then extended his loving creation of man when he put him to sleep, extracted a rib and then formed woman from it and placed the man and woman together as one. In his thoughtful and purposeful design God created an order.

That is the premise, however, it is with the understanding that man has fallen from the stature God created and intended for man in substance, spirit and portrayal (Romans 3:23). There are many historical factors that have influenced the current depiction of men within the different races, cultures and ethnic groups and a number of historical works that address them. The purpose of this work is to uplift men while acknowledging their shortcomings, and inspire and appeal to them to live up to their calling.

There are three categories of men alluded to in the book *Celebrating Men:* 1)Those who are predators, 2)Those who are protectors and 3)Those who are confused. Many men may identify with having been all three at different times in their lives, depending on their relationships, levels of maturity or spiritual experiences. There are many factors that influence a man to act in accordance with either category. *Celebrating Men* illuminates some of those factors. The ultimate portrait of man being presented will be that of a protector based on biblical teachings and examples. The text, *Celebrating Men*, uses the author's life experiences as case studies. The discussion guide, *Celebrating Men Companion,* is a tool that provides a forum to discuss the challenges presented and to help find biblical solutions.

For this discussion we will be using the following definitions for Celebration, Predator, Protector and Confused Men:

Celebrate - To extol or praise; to honor; to lift up.
Predators - According to the dictionary definition of a *Predator*; "a predator is an animal that lives by killing and consuming other animals." *Predatory* is described as: "Of or relating to plunder; disposed to exploit others; preying on other animals" (*Merriam-Webster Dictionary*). The working definition employed herein is that of preying upon and exploiting others.
Protectors - A guardian; one who guards or shields from injury (*Merriam-Webster Dictionary*). This definition is the one retained in our text, and
Confused - "To be mentally unclear or uncertain; to mix up: jumble" (*Merriam-Webster Dictionary*). Working definition in *Celebrating Men*: to be unsure of who you are or unclear of your role and purpose as a man.

This discussion guide is divided into three parts:
Part 1- Early Impressions of Manhood (Chapters 1-4),
Part 2-Young Adulthood (Chapters 5-7) and
Part 3- Becoming Mature (Chapters 8-12).

Each part includes a brief introduction summarizing that phase in the author's life, the development of her outlook on men and how those periods led to her ultimate choice to celebrate men. Read the introduction to each Part. The introductions are critical to setting the tone for the discussion questions. Before delving into the discussion questions in each chapter, it is highly recommended that the group read the daily confession as instructed.

Enjoy!

Part 1
Early Impressions of Manhood

Part 1
Introduction

Men, who are they, what role do they play or fulfill in the life of a child, a family and society? Can one man's influence override the influence of another during those early years of one's childhood? Why are men so important? Who says they are important?

Who is a dad? Where is my dad? Did I really ask all those questions as a child? Not in such an adult way, maybe, but the mind of a child is a curious one. It is during these early years that we form impressions of who we are and what we are meant to be. It is during these years that our identity is formed and strengthened. In Part One of *Celebrating Men,* B. Niles recounts experiences of men in her early childhood that laid the foundation for who she is today. The early impressions are the skeleton, the framework upon which everything else was built. As you go through the *Companion* and refer back to the book, consider how each experience shaped her thought process and influenced her sexuality. Regardless of some of the negative experiences in her early childhood, God placed a sufficient number of godly, uplifting and protective men in her life to counter the glum picture of men that could otherwise have formed.

Chapter One

First Impression of Manhood

"First impressions are constant in society…
Good ones are pleasant and long lasting,
Bad ones long and difficult to disprove."
~ Diego Velasquez

"Train a child in the way he should go
and when he is old he will not turn from it."
~ Proverbs 22:6

Y ou only have one chance to make a first impression on someone. In the case of children, however, I think they are much more forgiving and accommodating than adults if that first impression isn't a good one. In this first chapter, the author recounts her first impression of manhood through the example of her dad and mom and other dad-like figures that were present in her life through her childhood. She stresses the importance and lasting impact of the male parental figure on children whether the male parental figure is present or absent, whether his presence and influence is positive or negative.

The author included her mother's influence in this chapter because mothers aid in the shaping of their child's picture of manhood by how they treat and respond to their husbands or mates and by what they teach their young children about their fathers.

As you begin the journey of *Celebrating Men,* you might find it challenging at times to understand how the author is elevating men through some of the experiences and examples she shares. Note that it begins with the intent of the heart–to be obedient to

God and to uplift men. The premise of thought is that it is God's order and therefore the godly solution for better communities. God created men to be at the helm of the family. Each family affects the environment in their community and our world is made up of various communities.

The author employs the definitions below for the understanding of Celebration, Predator, Protector and Confused Men that will be used throughout this guide:

Celebrate - To extol or praise; to honor; to lift up.

Predators - According to the dictionary definition of a *Predator*; "a predator is an animal that lives by killing and consuming other animals." *Predatory* is described as: "Of or relating to plunder; disposed to exploit others; preying on other animals" (*Merriam-Webster Dictionary*). The working definition employed herein is that of preying upon and exploiting others.

Protectors - A guardian; one who guards or shields from injury (*Merriam-Webster Dictionary*). This definition is the one retained in our text, and

Confused - "To be mentally unclear or uncertain; to mix up: jumble" (*Merriam-Webster Dictionary*). Working definition in *Celebrating Men*: to be unsure of who you are, unclear of your role and purpose as a man.

Read/Recite the Daily Confession (Page 39)

Group Discussion
1. What role should a father play in the lives of their children and why? (Read Ephesians 6:4, Ephesians 5:1, 2 and Proverbs 22:6.)

2.   How would you describe the father in this chapter? (Was he predatory, was he protective, was he confused or a combination of all at different times?)

3. What possible rationalizations did the author give as reasons why her father may have acted as he did? (What was his background?)

4. What was this father's focus?

5. What are some ways the first impressions of manhood described in this chapter affected the author?

6. What were some of your first impressions of manhood?

Chapter Two
Innocent Trials

*"Count it all joy when you go through diverse trials,
because you know that the testing of your faith develops
perseverance."*
~ James 1:2, 3 (KJV)

It's often difficult to accept some of the hurtful deeds done to children. It is often difficult for us to see God's protection or love for us during those times. But we must trust in God's love and wisdom and walk by faith. In James 1:2-3, we are told to "count it all joy when you fall into various trials, knowing that the testing of your faith produces patience." As painful as even the experiences or "trials" that occur involving our children, we still have to apply the Word of God to it. How in the world can we "count it all joy" when the innocent are abused or taken advantage of? Yet if we trust God's omnipotence and omnipresence; if we trust that God is love; if we believe that God will do as he says and work all things together for our good; if we believe that God's ways and thoughts are so much higher than our ways and thoughts, even as high as the heavens are above the earth (Isaiah 55:8-9), then we will trust him even with our children. After all, they are His children first. They are only loaned to us.

We have to have a right perspective of our trials. We have to first recognize when they are trials or tests to be able to deal with them effectively.

Read/Recite the Daily Confession (Page 39)

Group Discussion

1. How are "Innocent Trials" described? (What is the author's definition of "Innocent Trials"?

2. Give an example of an "Innocent Trial" described in this chapter?

3. Are the characters in this chapter being predators, protectors or are they confused at this point?

4. Do you agree or disagree that the trials were innocent and why?

5. Do you agree that innocent trials are common or natural and if so, why?

6. How can "Innocent Trials" be damaging to children?

7. What are some ways to protect children from being victims of "Innocent Trials?" (Read Ephesians 6:10-18; 2 Corinthians 10:3-5.)

8. What are some ways parents, churches and schools can help to prevent abuse and educate families on this subject?

Chapter Three

My Super Hero

"...While we were still sinners,
Christ died for us."
~ Romans 5:8

Romans 5:8, "While we were still sinners, Christ died for us." God gave his only begotten Son for us before we even knew or cared of his existence. A hero is defined in *Webster* as "a mythological or legendary character of great strength or ability;" or "a man admired for his achievements and qualities." Though some hold that Jesus and the testimonies of his peers of his day were "mythological" or overly emphasized, there is actually enough evidence recorded, and a plethora of it from many sources, to justify his existence, the record of his birth, acts, death and resurrection regardless of how fantastic they sound. In fact, it is why he was crucified, because of how fantastic or unbelievable it all appeared to the Jews of his day and their jealousy and fear of their power being supplanted.

The life, death and resurrection of Jesus make him the most remarkable super hero of all time. No one else has done what Jesus has done or can do what Jesus can do today and forevermore.

Read/recite the Daily Confession (Page 39)

Group Discussion
1. Who is the author's super hero?

2. How do you define a super hero?

3. List a few reasons why the author calls him her super hero?

4. How does Jesus differ from the super heroes in our childhood or how does he differ from our current super heroes?
   a) In how he lived his life? (Read Matthew 20:20-28.)

   b) In how he helped or provided for others? (Read John 14:14-21, Mark 5:21-34, Matthew 9:27-34, Matthew 8:5-13.)

   c) In how he treated his enemies by example and in teaching? (Read Matthew 5:43-48; Matthew 26:21-26, 47-50; Luke 23:32-43.)

   d) In how he saved lives? (Read Romans 5:8, John 15:13.)

   e) In his deliverance? (i.e., is it temporary or permanent?) (John 3:16; 1 John 5:11-12)

5. Are super heroes typically predators or protectors?

6. Who is your super hero and why?

Chapter Four

Tender Teens

"How can a young man keep his way pure?
By living according to your word."
~ Psalms 119:9

King David was a boy when God first anointed him and used him. (Read 1 Samuel 16:5-13; 1 Timothy 4:12- 5:2.) It is David who wrote most of the Psalms and wrote the Psalm at the heading of this chapter. Timothy was possibly a teenager when he entered the ministry with Paul. The teen years are special and impressionable.

In this chapter the author gives several examples of young men that made an impact in shaping her outlook on men and her own personal development during her early teen years. The term tender is used in the sense of "delicate," developing or even in an "immature" sense as defined in *Webster's Dictionary*. Sensitive and impressionable can be added to complete the definition as it is being used in this chapter. These are still formative years in a young person's sexuality and outlook on life. In many cultures, it is during this period that a boy or girl goes through rites of passages into manhood or womanhood. The Jews have the Bar Mitzvah; many Latin American countries have the "Quinceñera" for girls. Western culture has the "Sweet Sixteen" or the Cotillion. Some Asian and African cultures have arranged marriages that take place at thirteen and fourteen years of age.

The teen years are when girls and boys start to "find themselves." They go through a lot of hormonal changes and have to learn how to accept, control and manage these changes.

It's a special time in their lives. In the Bible we see examples of young kings and heroes that emerge during their teen years. We find that this period the author calls "Tender Teens," was pivotal for her as well.

Read/Recite the Daily Confession (Page 39)

Group Discussion
1. Why do you think the author titled this chapter, "Tender Teens?"

2. Give examples of predatory, protective and confused men in this chapter and why you think they fall in that category (or categories).

3. Based on descriptions given, what do you think could have been some of the factors that made the difference between some taking predatory roles and some protective roles?

4. What insight can you gain about young women from the author's experiences?

5. As a man (teen or adult), what are some things you think you can do to make a difference or impact the tender teens in your life and community?

Part 2
Young Adulthood

Part 2
Introduction

In the next few chapters of *Celebrating Men* the author is like a blossoming flower in spring. As spring time is full of new beginnings and discoveries, so too, the author is discovering how, as a young woman, to interact with young men on different levels. It's a time in life when one has just finished high school and is entering college, or just finished college and is seeking a career. It's a time of exploration and discovery; it's a time of trial and error. During period in the author's life, she learns who her true "brothers" are. She also goes through a period of disillusionment and rebellion against God and finally learns how to develop godly friendships with men.

As you review this section in the book, consider the lessons the author is learning. Consider this stage in your own life and what factors influenced or are influencing your young adult attitudes and philosophies of life. It is during this period that we make some very important choices that can channel the direction of our lives for decades.

Chapter Five

Who Are My Brothers?

There is a destiny that makes us brothers,
no one goes his way alone;
all that we send into the lives of others,
comes back into our own.
~ Edwin Markham

In this chapter on "Who Are My Brothers?," the author gives biblical explanation for who Jesus said our brothers are and highlights examples from her life of those who acted as brothers on her behalf and those who did not. She emphasizes that acting brotherly is not limited to biological brothers or even brothers in faith, but by those who demonstrate brotherhood, not unlike the good Samaritan in Jesus' parable when he was asked, "who is my neighbor" in Luke 10:27-37.

Read/Recite the Daily Confession (Page 39)

Group Discussion
1. Read Matthew 12:48-50 and Luke 10:27-37.

2. How are these two passages similar?

3. Who did Jesus say are our brothers in 12:48-50?

4. How does a brother behave?

5. In this chapter, who were true brothers to the author and why do you think so?

6. According to the author, how do many Christian women feel about their Christian brothers? Do they generally feel protected or as prey?

7. The author asks the question, "Does it always have to be about courtship or dating?" Do you believe it's difficult to be strictly "brotherly" with women; if so, why?

8. Read 1 Thessalonians 4:3-6 and discuss the meaning and implications.

9. What are some examples the author gives in the following paragraph of how men can demonstrate brotherly conduct?

   "Most women are waiting for you to take the lead as a man and show them how a man can control his own body in holiness and honor. But even more importantly, can you show her honor? Can you deny yourself? Can you overlook her ignorance or lack of self-respect and give her respect, because after all, she is a vessel for which Christ died."

10. What do you find to be some of the challenges to behaving brotherly towards your sister in Christ?

11. What are some of the strategies you can use to overcome those challenges and become more brotherly to women?

Chapter Six
Turning Point

"It is never too late to become what you might have been."
~ George Elliot

"That if you confess with your mouth, 'Jesus is Lord'
and believe in your heart
that God raised him from the dead,
you will be saved."
~ Romans 10:9

Thank God for his mercy and his grace or none of us would have access to the Kingdom of God. Thank God that he gives second, third, and fourth chances. He says in 1 Corinthians 13 that love keeps no record of wrongs and we know based on other Scripture references that God is love. That is why we can go to him and confess our sins, without count, and he is faithful and just to forgive us and purify us of all unrighteousness (1 John 1:9).

This chapter recounts a turning point in the author's rebellion against God. She was angry with God and his people and this led her to leave his protective covering, but her heart wasn't far from him. Examine how this is expressed in this chapter through the ensuing questions.

Read/Recite the Daily Confession (Page 39)

Group Discussion
    (Read John 3:17, Romans 8:1)
    1. What was the turning point the author describes that
        occurred in her life?

2. How would you describe Brett and Henry's behavior towards the author? Was it predatory, protective or confused?

3. Do you believe that the three examples/incidents given in this chapter are common and if so why?

4. What caused the author to turn back to God?

5. If she had not turned back to God during this critical period, what other directions do you think her life could have taken? (Explore that.)

6. What are some biblical examples of men or women that had some major turning points in their lives? (Examples: John 18:15-27; Acts 9:1-20.)

Chapter Seven

Friendship Training

"Hold a true friend with both your hands."
~ Nigerian Proverb

"Faithful are the wounds of a friend;
but the kisses of an enemy are deceitful."
~ Proverbs 27:6

Friendship is a broad term. In this chapter friendship between men and women is being explored and encouraged. The author believes that developing godly friendships with the opposite sex are healthy and can actually help prepare one for a healthy marriage relationship.

Read/Recite the Daily Confession (Page 39)

Group Discussion

1. Discuss the meaning of Proverbs 27:6.

2. Do you believe in friendships with the opposite sex?

3. Did you find some of the examples of the author's friendships given in this chapter challenging to your concept of friendship? If so, how? (See example of Raul – page 59-61.)

4. Who were the key men in this chapter that *significantly* impacted the author's life and helped to shape her

outlook on friendships with the opposite sex? Put a
check mark by your choices below and discuss why.

Barry ____	Kevin ____
Ian ____	Sean ____
Karl ____	Gregory ____
Tevon ____	Raul ____

5. How does the author expect to be treated and do you
    think this is common or uncommon of single women in
    America?

6. What reasons does the author give for the challenge of
    getting through to some independent, seemingly self-
    sufficient women? (See pages 49-50 in *Celebrating
    Men*.)

7. What lesson(s) did the author learn by refraining from
    dating?

8. How does she define general and specific purpose?

9. Identify in the passages below, whether it relates to
    general or specific purpose or both.

John 4:23	John 17:11, 20-23
Matt. 9:1-8	John 3:16
Romans 12:1	2 Timothy 1:16-18
2 Timothy 1:6	Acts 10:1-23

10. What point is the author trying to make in the following
    paragraph: "Just because a man and a woman find each
    other attractive doesn't mean they have to move into a
    dating relationship"?

11. How do you define friendship?

Part 3
Becoming Mature

Part 3
Introduction

In order to become mature in our faith, according to James
1:2-4, our faith must be tested. He says that, "…you know that
the testing of your faith develops perseverance. Perseverance
must finish its work so that you may be mature and complete,
not lacking anything." At the end of most classes and courses
there are exams designed to test the strength of our
understanding of the material covered in the class. So too in life
we go through tests that reveal our level of understanding and
continue our developmental process. If we fail, we end up
repeating the lessons over and over again until we can pass the
tests and become mature.

Thus far in *Celebrating Men* the author's mindset concerning
relationships with men was being shaped and solidified. She
was going through a process of self-development and learning
about the secular versus biblical and godly dynamics of
male/female relationships that would govern the rest of her life.

The author's experiences in the last section of the book test her
stand and the strength of her faith. The following chapters
demonstrate some subtle ways in which Satan can insinuate
himself into our lives. He uses tactics designed to destroy us,
get us off track and out of God's will. In each of the following
chapters the author is either in a relationship or being tempted
with one. Each case presents itself with subtle spiritual attacks
to undermine her stand for purity or to pull her out of obedience

to God's will. Each experience not only tests her stand and belief, but strengthens her in the process.

Chapter Eight
Undisciplined

"Brave is the lion tamer, brave is the world subduer,
but braver is the one who has subdued himself."
~ Johann Gottfried Von Herder

"Like a city whose walls are broken down,
is a man who lacks self-control."
~ Proverbs 25:28

This chapter is a bit touchy. The author in this chapter is equating undisciplined behavior with weakness. Being described as undisciplined is more palatable than being described as weak, yet she alludes to undisciplined men, in particular those who cannot control their sexual desire, as weak men. How is this chapter aligned with the theme of this book in celebrating men? There is a saying, "It is better to build a boy than repair a man." Along those same lines is the common knowledge that it is better to expose, clean and treat a wound so that it can heal than to ignore it and allow it to fester and become a larger wound.

Scripture encourages us to "speak the truth in love," to "confess our sins to one another" and that if a brother offends you or sins against you to go and confront that brother (Matthew 18:15-17). The purpose of this instruction is to edify or to build us up. The good, the bad and the ugly has to be addressed for maturity and healing to occur. None of us are perfect. The undesirable, the unattractive and the ugly part of us must also be addressed and purged so that we can come forth as gold. The sexually undisciplined Christian man (or woman) hurts people including themselves. They cause deep wounds in the body of Christ and this must be addressed in order for men (and women) to mature in Christ and for our men to be celebrated as they want to be and ought to be.

The author repeatedly quotes Romans 12:2 in various parts of the book, "Do not conform any longer to the pattern of this world, but be transformed by the renewing of your mind." In the world men applaud each other and are celebrated for their sexual prowess. In Christ it is the opposite. So though this subject is a bit bitter to the taste in light of the subject of celebrating men, it is nevertheless an intricate part of the author's theme. A major theme in the book *Celebrating Men* is that the author is celebrating those men who have had the discipline and regard to protect her sexually. She is also making an appeal for more men to recognize, identify and fix or strengthen the weak areas in their lives, the areas in their "walls" that are broken down.

Read/Recite the Daily Confession (Page 39)

Group Discussion
1. How is strength defined in this chapter?

2. Do you agree with the author's definition of strength? Explain why or why not.

3. In the example of Jason given in this chapter, does he have a predatory, protective or confused mindset and why?

4. What do you think of the author's suggested, alternative response to the movie she watched with Jason? (See page 69.)

5. Was Lenny being a predator, protector or was he confused and why?

6. The author stated that she did not "cut off" communication with Lenny after discerning his predatory or confused nature (Page 72, 3rd paragraph). How might things have worked out differently if she had?

7. Review the three questions at the end of Chapter eight in the text.

8. How does this chapter's citing of undisciplined men, still celebrate men?

Chapter Nine
The Deceptiveness of the Gradual

*"All deception in the course of life
is indeed nothing else but a lie reduced to practice,
and falsehood passing from words into things."*
~ Robert Southey

This chapter continues in the vein of developing maturity of faith, being discerning of Satan's strategies to cause us to settle or fall and being alert to our human weaknesses. We make decisions every day. What we often think of as small decisions can collectively equal a huge decision or direction for our lives. If we are not alert to this pattern in life, we will be tossed to and fro by life. The purpose driven life is one that is directed by a sum of purposeful decisions to reach a desired end.

The author in this chapter expresses her awareness of this principle but didn't have the discipline to completely comply with it in this case study. Nevertheless, she felt it worthy of inclusion in the book because it is such a common occurrence in many lives and another tactic of the enemy of which to be aware. The gentleman (and men like him) in the chapter is still one that she admires, celebrates and thinks worthy of esteem, but the purpose of the chapter is to expose the subtlety with which we can get off track or out of God's will and the consequences thereof. We are exhorted repeatedly in Scripture to "be alert" or in some translations, "sober" (1 Peter 5:8; 1:13; 1 Thessalonians 5:6) because it's too easy to fall asleep. It's too easy to get comfortable, to be lured in gradually and trapped in a relationship, situation or sin and many a man (and woman) has fallen for the trap and lost their way. Be sober; be alert.

Read/Recite the Daily Confession (Page 39)

Group Discussion
1. What do you perceive is the purpose of this chapter?

2. How can one be gradually deceived according to the author?

3. What, if anything, was wrong with TJ?

4. Was TJ a predator, protector or confused? Justify your answer.

5. What about this chapter celebrates men?

6. What did the author learn from the experience of this relationship?

7. Give some examples in Scripture, life or personally of being gradually deceived and the effects of it. (Example: King Saul, obesity, sin)

Chapter Ten
Disbelief, Disobedience & Downfall

*"The purpose of problems is to push you toward obedience to
God's laws, which are exact and cannot be changed.
We have the free will to obey them or disobey them.
Obedience will bring harmony,
disobedience will bring you more problems."
~ Peace Pilgrim Quotes*

Sometimes we are simply drawn away by our own lust.
(Read James 1:13-15 and 1 John 2:15, 16.) We know what is
right but we may be in a spiritually weakened state because of a
lack of prayer and slackness in studying the Word of God. We
may be discouraged or lonely and more easily susceptible to
temptation. However, when God has taken the time to warn us
of impending attack or to prepare us for a time of testing and we
fail to heed the warning, we can be destroyed, seriously injured
or grossly side-tracked.

In this chapter on "Disbelief, Disobedience and Downfall," the
author shares a personal example of how God forewarned her,
via a dream, of a time of tempting that was coming and the
consequences if she failed to resist the temptation. God wasn't
leading her into the temptation; he knew it was coming and
wanted her to be prepared. He also told her that she could
prevent the undesirable outcome. It was serious enough for God
to forewarn her as a way of preparation. But because of
disbelief, she stumbled and fell.

When we yield to lust, it becomes like a heavy weight around
our neck. The Bible says in Galatians 6:8, "The one who sows
to please his sinful nature from that nature will reap
destruction..." If you are going to live a life of integrity before

God and man, it starts with a spirit of humility and obedience. (Read 1 Samuel 15:22-23.) Take heed and save yourself a lot of heartache, strife and loss. The author lost her home and intimacy with God for a season. The answers to her prayers were delayed due to her disobedience and she almost ruined her testimony.

Read/Recite the Daily Confession (Page 39)

Group Discussion
(Read 1 Corinthians 9:24-27.)
1. Why did the author disbelieve the dream?

2. What can we learn about God because of the dream?

3. In the example given, what strategy did Satan use to lure the author into sin?

4. Did the author eventually overcome the temptation and if so, how?

5. What are some similar strategies that the enemy uses to try to trap you?

6. What are some defensive or offensive strategies you can use to counter the enemy's darts?

7. In this example, was Sam acting as a predator, a protector or as a confused man?

8. Is the author still celebrating him and if so, how?

Chapter Eleven
Job (Why Lord?)

"The capacity to be puzzled is the premise of all creation,
Be it in art or in science" or otherwise.
~ Erich Fromm

W hy is it so difficult at times to "Trust in the Lord with all your heart and lean not on your own understanding...?" (Read Proverbs 3:5-6.) There are going to be times in our lives when we just don't understand certain circumstances and are not meant to, at least not at that time. Like a parent who has quantum more experience and knowledge than his five or ten-year-old child and directs his child in ways for his or her protection and good, so too, our Father God, directs and commands us. As the five-year-old has no clue or understanding of their father's directive, so we often may have no clue or understanding of the work God is doing in and through us. Yet God expects us to obey him even as an earthly father expects his children to obey him.

Because we consider ourselves as adults to be knowledgeable or "grown," we sometimes question the workings of God and choose to follow our own logic. In this chapter, the author was emerging out of a period of spiritual wilderness when she entered into the relationship with Cedric. The stress of the relationship drew her back to her knees and renewed intimacy with the Lord. Though God guided her through the season with Cedric, she never quite attained clarity as to why she had to go through the experience. She just had to trust the Lord and not lean on her own understanding. She acknowledged him in all her ways and God did direct her paths as though through a maze. Maybe when she's a little more "grown" God will reveal to her the reason for the experience.

Read/Recite the Daily Confession (Page 39)

Group Discussion

1. What was so puzzling about Cedric?

2. Was he a predator, protector or confused? Explain.

3. How did God show his loving care in this example?

4. Have you ever wondered why God allows certain situations in your life? Give an example.

5. What perspective should we employ in difficult situations we don't understand or when we haven't received clear revelation from the Lord as to the purpose of the difficult situations?

6. In this chapter the author reiterates the difference between God's specific and general purposes for our lives. What specific purpose do you think Cedric could have served in her life?

7. The example of Cedric reveals some good character traits and some shady ones. Was the example of Cedric that of a protector, a predator or a confused man? (Please explain.)

Chapter Twelve
Good is the Enemy of Best

"To obey is better than sacrifice."
~ 1 Samuel 15:22

What is good versus what is best for an individual is what this chapter explores. The author gives several different situations of good versus personal and spiritual best and then compares them to God's best and God's will. We all have different tastes, different interests, ideals and different types of people that we find attractive. So where or how do we come to a common standard of what is best? Is that possible or even necessary?

It is the belief of the author that everything points back to God's word and God's will. Once again we are directed back to Romans 12:2 which says, "Do not conform any longer to the pattern of this world, but be transformed by the renewing of your mind. Then you will be able to test and approve what God's will is-his good, pleasing and perfect will." "There is a way that seems right to man but in the end it leads to death" (Proverbs 16:25). Our good is not God's good. Our best is not God's best unless it's in alignment with his will and purposes.

As we conclude with this final chapter in *Celebrating Men*, it is important to remember as men (and women) of God, the height of God's creation and joint-heirs with Christ, that as we strive to be vessels of honor and celebrated beings, it can only be fully attained in and through the blood of Jesus Christ. It can only be attained as we walk in obedience to his Holy Spirit.

Read/Recite the Daily Confession (Page 39)

Group Discussion

1. What does the author mean by "good is the enemy of best"?

2. Was the example of Craig that of a predator, protector or a confused man? Explain why.

3. Was Craig someone that the author celebrated? Why or why not?

4. What are some examples of good being the enemy of best in our lives?

5. How can the knowledge of this principle help you to become the man (or woman) God wants you to be?

6. In the examples below, discuss whether the characters chose what was good or what was best in their situation and explain why.
   - Genesis 12:1-9   - Genesis 15:2-6, 16:1-4
   - Ruth 1:6-18; 2:1-12   - 1 Samuel 15:1-9
   - Mark 14:3-5   - Acts 4:52 – 5:2

7. What are some ways or signs that can help you discern whether you've chosen what is best versus what is good?

Daily Confession:

I am a new creature in Christ, old things are passed
away and behold all things have become new.
(2 Cor. 10:17)

"**T**herefore, there is now no condemnation for those
who are in Christ Jesus because through Christ
Jesus the law of the Spirit of life set me free from
the law of sin and death."
(Romans 8:1, 2)

If I sin, he said: "If we confess our sins, he is
faithful and just to forgive us of all our sins and
purify us from all unrighteousness."
(1 John 1:9)

So then, I do not conform any longer to the pattern
of this world. I am being transformed by the
renewing of my mind so that I may test and approve
what God's will is, his good, pleasing and perfect will.
(Romans 12:2)